MARC CHAGALL

AVEC L'AUTORISATION DE A. MAEGHT, ED.

FELICITAS TOBIEN

MARC CHAGALL

Artline Editions

Translated by Stephen Gorman

© 1988 by Berghaus Verlag – D 8347 Kirchdorf/Inn
English Language Rights: Artlines UK Ltd, 2 Castle Street,
Thornbury, Bristol. Avon, England
Printed in West Germany – Imprimé en Allemagne
ISBN 1 871487 00 5

CONTENTS

"When Chagall paints, one is not sure if he is asleep or if he is awake. He must have an angel somewhere in his head."

It was no one less than Pablo Picasso who attempted to describe the phenomenon Chagall in this way, and his words correspond to what Chagall once said of himself. "I am a painter and an unconsciously conscious painter so to speak."

This "unconscious consciousness", this condition between imagination and reality, as well as a masterly feeling for colour, was virtually the source from which works full of artistic poetry sprung. Art was for Chagall "above all a frame of mind", and so it was only natural that memories of his Russian homeland flowed into his paintings again and again, memories which sometimes reached back to his early childhood. One could regard him to a certain extent as an envoy of Russia, but also as a mediator of Chassidism, the Jewish religious doctrine of Eastern Europe. But this would only emphasize one aspect of this many sided productive artist.

When Marc Chagall was born on July 7th, 1887 in Witebsk, a town in White Russia with then approximately 50.000 inhabitants, he seemed to have been born under an unlucky star. In his autobiography "My Life", he describes himself as "stillborn" and relates that someone at first "pricked him with needles" and "dipped him in a bucket of water" before he was eventually able to give "a weak whimper". In addition to this, a fire had broken out in the neighbourhood at exactly the time of his birth. It quickly spread so that mother and child had to be brought without delay "to a safe place at the other end of town".

A dramatic prelude, and Chagall commented later tongue in cheek, "... I hope that the psychologists do not draw undue conclusions from this ..."

After these initial difficulties, his further development ran smoothly, although the life of the pious Jewish family was determined by poverty.

Marc was the oldest of nine children and was actually called Mosche Segal. His mother ran a small general store, his father was employed in a herring warehouse where he had to work very hard for little money. "Hellish work, galley-slave work," said the son about the job which his father did every day, without complaint, in order that he could feed his family. "He carried heavy barrels, and my heart bent like a Turkish pretzel when I saw him lifting these loads and rummaging around in the little herrings with his icy hands," Chagall remembered. He was full of admiration as well as loving affection and respect for his hardworking, thrifty parents who sacrificed so much so that he and his brothers and sisters always had enough to eat. "There was always enough butter and cheese on the table. Sandwiches, like a permanent symbol, never disappeared from my hands as a child."

Marc Chagall first went to the Jewish primary school and then changed to the official parish school — something which was only allowed to Jews in exceptional cases. His first artistic inclinations were already obvious. He began to play the violin and started to draw, took singing lessons with the choir leader of the synagogue and applied successfully to be his aide. "... on the important holidays, I listened together with the whole synagogue to my melodious soprano. I saw smiling faces and attentiveness among the faithful, and I dreamt: I will become a singer, the leader of a choir. I will attend the academy of music."

He did not keep these intentions for long. Soon he secretly saw himself as a violinist, a dancer, a poet ...

In any case he wanted "a special profession" which "would not force him to turn away from heaven and the stars." Art presented itself. His hands were "too tender" anyway to move barrels like his father did, as he found out with relief.

Wishing and carrying out his wishes were of course two completely different things. In those days, artists were not exactly commonplace in Witebsk, in fact Chagall believed no one before him had uttered the words "art" and "artist" in his hometown. He could therefore expect little understanding from his relatives.

Once when he showed his mother a picture which he had painted and hopefully asked, "See, Mama, do you like it", she is supposed to have viewed his painting "with God knows what eyes" and eventually answered hesitatingly, "Yes, my son, I see you have talent. But listen, my child, perhaps you would rather be a shop-assistant ..."

By chance Chagall discovered one day in town a notice with the heading "Pen's Painting and Drawing School". He accepted this as fate and decided to join this school. It was not easy to make it palatable to his mother who had the say in the house, but Marc was persistent, and eventually she agreed that he was allowed to go to Pen, first of all to introduce himself.

Chagall rolled his "crumpled drawings" together. His mother accompanied him to Pen's studio, she wanted to hear his opinion with her own ears.

Jehuda Pen had studied at the Petersburg Academy. He painted portraits and genre pictures in the style of the official salons of the turn of the century. Marc Chagall described his first

Table I

Summery Lunch Hour
From the cycle Daphne and Chloe. 1961
Colour lithograph, 42 x 32 cm

decisive steps on the way to his artistic future, "By going up his steps, I was already enclouded and intoxicated with the smell of the paint and the pictures." A brief glance at the paintings which lay around was enough to make him realize though that he did not want to paint like this forever, but he was happy to be accepted as a pupil. "Yes, he has talent," Jehuda Pen had said and so dispelled the worries of the parents to some extent.

He attended Pen's studio for about two months. At the same time he worked as a retoucher with a photographer. He was, however, not very happy with his job. "I did not see why one had to hide these spots, wrinkles, and folds, or rejuvenate all the different, lifeless figures ..." He prematurely finished his apprenticeship, although his master had prophesied a "brilliant future", and in the winter of 1906/07 he went to St Petersburg instead together with his friend Viktor Mekler to study painting.

It was an adventurous undertaking. Firstly, as a Jew, one needed a special residence permit, as the Czar had decreed a certain district which Jews were not allowed to leave, and secondly, Chagall did not know how he was to exist in the future. The 27 roubles which his father had given him as he started on his journey would soon be used up. How was he going to make money in the big strange city?

When worries of that sort threatened to overcome him, he told himself, „Most important is art, painting, a style of painting which is completely different to what other people do." With this aim in mind he hoped to be able to master all the difficulties better. But sometimes he was frightened by his own courage. "Will God or someone else give me the strength to breathe new life into my paintings, the breath of prayer and mourning, the prayer of redemption and rebirth?"

In moments like this he felt small and helpless like a child, and his start in St Petersburg did not exactly raise his self-confidence. His attempt to be accepted for the Baron Steglitz School of Arts and Crafts was unsuccessful. Chagall failed the entrance examination. He did not have any choice but to be satisfied with a less exclusive school — the school of the "Imperial Society for the Promotion of Art" where he was accepted without any test for the third class. Later he remembered this time with mixed feelings. "Innumerable plaster heads of Greek and Roman citizens stared at me from each corner, and I as a poor provincial had to involve myself with the horrible nostrils of Alexander of Macedonia or another plaster idiot ..."

Although he did not feel that he gained any decisive profit from the tuition, he was at least successful in finding acknowledgement for his work, and eventually he could number himself among the scholarship-holders which meant that he had 10 roubles per month at his disposal for one year. Up until then he had struggled through by taking temporary jobs. Now life became more bearable, at last he had enough to eat again.

One problem remained: he still had no residence permit. He had travelled to St Petersburg with a temporary certificate which his father had obtained for him and had from then on wrangled his way through, something which had not been easy and not without danger. To put an end to the constant fear of being caught, he decided to learn a trade which would give him "the right of abode in the capital". He started an apprenticeship with a sign-maker.

As Chagall felt that the school of the "Imperial Society for the Promotion of Art" was more obstructive than helpful for his artistic development, he looked around for another school and was successful. In the summer of 1908, he was able to transfer to the Svanseva School which was run by the painter and stage-designer Léon Bakst. Bakst was a renowned artistic personality and his institute — the only one in St Petersburg "inspired by the European spirit" — was even attended by the nobility. All this impressed the 21 year old, but at the same time he was intimidated. As an exceptionally sensitive young painter, he was incredibly embarrassed when Bakst criticized him in front of the others. Once he was so grieved that he stayed away from the school for three months to "orientate himself in freedom" before he again placed himself under the severe judgement of the tutor. Soon, however, Bakst was completely convinced of Marc Chagall's talent and was increasingly full of praise. He found the most suitable wording with his comment, "Now your colours are singing," as the Chagall colours stood out relatively early because of their fascinating character. They were full of life and as pure as the euphony of a human voice.

1910 brought about a fateful turn in Chagall's life. He had hardly seen anything of the world apart from Witebsk and St Petersburg. Léon Bakst wanted to leave the city for good and Marc found that under these circumstances there was no reason for him to remain in St Petersburg any longer. He asked his tutor to take him to Paris. Bakst agreed and even gave him some money, but for some unknown reason this joint trip never took place. The Paris plan was, however, maintained although Chagall anticipated that leaving Russia would not be easy for him. "... I realized that I had to go. But I had difficulty in making clear to myself what I wanted. I must admit that I was too much of a provincial," he wrote in his memoirs and admitted that he enjoyed moving town but ultimately he only dreamed "of being alone in a cage".

He started out for France in autumn 1910. A patron had bought several pictures from him and also promised him a monthly allowance so that he was provided with a moderate start in life.

"I left the country of my birth in 1910. At that time I was convinced that I needed Paris," he later said. "The ground which had nourished the roots of my art was Witebsk; but my art needed Paris — as a tree needs water — otherwise it would have withered away. I did not have any other reason for leaving my homeland to which I believe I have remained true in my art (in spite of everything). As an artist and a common man (I regard the common people as the most sensitive social class) I felt that plastic refinements of the highest degree only existed in France. I reached Paris with the thoughts, the dreams which only a twenty-year old can have; but perhaps I have retained these dreams for a long time. I was filled with enthusiasm for what I saw. But my enthusiasm returned to its starting point. By taking part in that unique technical revolution of art in France, I went, as it were, back to my own country in spirit. I lived as if I had turned backwards, looking forward."

In the beginning he was very homesick, and if the distance had not been so great, he would have left France again. But then the treasures of French art drew him under their spell. He found a second home in the museums and galleries of Paris.

He was overwhelmed as he stood in front of the paintings of the old masters for the first time, in front of works from the Impressionists, the Nabis, Fauves, and all those who, up until then, he had only known by name. He was especially impressed by the intensity of colour used by van Gogh and the Fauves. Suddenly Russian painting appeared heavy-handed to him. It seemed to him as if it was damned "to remain always in the tow of the West."

Chagall established a studio in Montparnasse, but in the following year moved to a larger house, "La Ruche" — in English "Beehive". "La Ruche", which was in the vicinity of the abattoirs of Vaugirard, accomodated approximately one hundred studios inhabited by "Bohemian artists from all over the world". Here he met Léger, Delaunay, Modigliani, Soutine, the poets Cendrars and Apollinaire and many more. Soon a deep friendship existed between him and some of them. His creative urge was untiring. Everything that he could lay his hands on and which was more or less usable was converted into a canvas: tablecloths and bedsheets as well as torn night shirts.

He did not attend an art school anymore because he knew that no academy could give him what he discovered when he visited exhibitions, galleries, and museums or when he wandered through the streets and squares in Paris to pursue his studies there. "The whole city was my tutor, in everything. The market traders, the waiters, the hotel porters, the farmers, the labourers. They were surrounded by that incredible atmosphere of enlightened freedom ('lumière-liberté'), which I had not found anywhere else."

Among Chagall's works from the early years in Paris one finds "The Holy Cab-Driver", "The Poet Mazin", "Homage to Apollinaire", "The Soldier Drinks", "Me and the Village", and "The Violinist in the Snow", one of those paintings whose central theme — the violinist — interested and inspired the artist time and time again.

At that time Paris was the centre of contemporary art, as it were, the scene of experiment in new theories and technique. Chagall eagerly absorbed everything which French art had to offer. Through this he intensified and furthered his gift for observation, and although he did not allow himself to be influenced to the extent that he renounced his individual way of painting, he eventually developed a new style. Several of his works from that time have cubist tendencies, while remaining typically Chagall, a synthesis of Jewish mysticism and cheerful composure, of Russian folk art and French progressiveness.

An example of the change which Chagall was undergoing is the "Self-Portrait with Seven Fingers" (1911/12), a masterly achievement of the 24 year-old. "Why seven fingers? In order to do it differently: Imagination next to reality. The dissonance increases the spiritual shock," he said.

No less worthy of note and unusual for the conditions at that time is his work "To Russia, to the Donkeys and to the Others" (1911/12). In the right half of the painting a woman with a milk bucket floats over the roofs of the city. Her head is detached from her body, the eyes look expectantly towards heaven. Chagall who stressed that a painting was for him "a large area with objects which are arranged in a certain way" maintained later that he had "separated the head from the body" because he "needed an empty space exactly in that spot."

This explanation could be accepted as genuine if Chagall's "Drunkard" (1911/12) did not also exist — so to speak as contradictory evidence — where the head has also been separated from the body. So it becomes obvious that it was not just the desire for an empty space which moved him to such a trick but rather more that the artist used it as an important form of expression. While the head of the drinker already leans towards the bottle and the mouth is open to drink, the hands and the headless body leaning away from the bottle convey the conflict in which the person finds himself.

Table II

Flight of the Cicade
From the cycle Daphne and Chloe. 1961
Colour lithograph, 42 x 32 cm

In the beginning his works appeared a little strange to the French, and Chagall thought to himself, "... perhaps my art is ... the art of a madman, a sparkling mercury, a blue spirit which closes in over my paintings," but he knew well enough that he should not make any concessions, that he had to remain an individualist as before, i.e. consequently continue on his chosen path and keep his distinct style. Once he had made an exception — in the hope of selling something on the market as his colleagues did — and attempted to paint "a landscape à la Corot". Since then he had learnt his lesson. He had found out: "The more I tried to paint a Corot, the more I became removed from it, and in the end it was a Chagall!"

Of course he wanted to exhibit his work. An individual exhibition in Paris was unthinkable as such a privilege was almost exclusively reserved to Matisse and Bonnard, so Chagall tried very hard to take part in the "Salon des Indépendants". This attempt was successful for the first time in 1911 but at the last minute it came to an unexpected incident. The paintings were already hanging on the wall, the exhibition was to be opened in an hour, when suddenly the accusation was made by the jury that one of the paintings was pornographic. Chagall had great difficulty preventing it from being removed — as the censor had demanded.

The poets Blaise Cendrars and Guillaume Apollinaire were among the first to recognize Chagall's genius. They were important companions during those years in Paris. Apollinaire, the inspirer of cubism and pioneer of surrealism, declared in view of Chagall's works that they were "surnaturel". Later he chose to describe them as "surreal" before the actual "surrealism" was born. "Chagall is a very talented artist and devotes himself to everything which his mystic and pagan imagination drives him to: his art is very sensual," commented Apollinaire and did not hesitate to introduce the Russian to Herwarth Walden, the influential patron of expressionist art. Walden always had an open ear where young talent was concerned. So he already took three paintings from Marc Chagall in 1913 — the year of their acquaintance — for the "First German Autumn Exhibition", and in 1914 he dedicated an individual exhibition to the artist in his gallery "Sturm" in Berlin.

Chagall travelled to the opening. Afterwards he continued his journey to Russia where he intended to stay for three months. The outbreak of World War I thwarted his plans. The intended three months became eight years. "When I was in Berlin, I did not foresee that one month later this bloody comedy would begin in whose course the whole world and with it Chagall would turn into a new theatrical scene of action, where enormous mass scenes would take place. No intuition warned me or stopped me from undertaking a trip to Russia ...; on the other hand I wanted to see 'her' again ..." "She" was Bella Rosenfeld, the daughter of a jeweller in Witebsk.

Chagall had met Bella in 1909 and had secretly regarded her as his bride for a long time. His humble origin was, however, a thorn in the sides of the rich jeweller family. Bella's family wished a more suitable match for their daughter, and Marc faced a lot of resentment. "He will never be able to earn his daily bread. You will perish with him, my child," warned mother Rosenfeld, "perish for no reason whatsoever. Apart from that he is an artist ..." But Bella bravely stood by him, she loved Marc, and so the wedding actually took place on July 25th, 1915 — in spite of all the prejudices. Their daughter Ida was born in the following year.

The happiness of the young marriage gave Chagall extra creative strength. Bella was his muse, the "model" for his art. "I never complete a painting or an etching without asking her for her yes or no," he admitted enthusiastically. Joy of life and love shone from the pictures of this time, and Bella served as a model again and again. Chagall painted her even after her death.

At first the family happiness distracted somewhat from the daily world affairs. But the dramatic developments could not be ignored for long. There could be no immediate return to France, and in Russia there was the threat of being called up for military service. To avoid serving on the front, Chagall worked in his brother-in-law's office which dealt with important military matters and thus formed an alternative to service on the front. He described the office as a "haven" which "the war had intended" for him.

Although Russia had not realized Chagall's true greatness, he was honoured with exhibitions in Moscow and St Petersburg during the war years. After the October Revolution all previous restrictions for Jews were lifted virtually over night. On September 12th, 1918, Anatoli Lunatscharski, the new head of the Ministry of Culture, appointed Chagall — whom he knew from Paris — commissioner for pictorial art in the district of Witebsk. There were various tasks connected with this appointment which the artist conscientiously carried out with a great expenditure of work. He organized exhibitions, opened museums, was responsible for the festivities in honour of the first anniversary of the October Revolution and founded an art academy in his town of which he became director. Chagall engaged famous tutors, for example El Lissitzky and Kasimir Malevitsch. His ardent desire was to bring art closer to the Russian people. He said, confident in the success of his efforts, "Believe me, the converted working people will be ready to ascend the peak of art and culture."

Unquestionably Chagall took his task seriously. "Clothed in a Russian smock, with a leather briefcase under my arm, I certainly gave the impression of being a Soviet functionary. Only the long hair and the pink on my cheeks from my paintings betrayed the artist. An administrative fire glowed in my eyes. I am surrounded by boys, students who I plan to turn into geniuses within 24 hours. I slave and toil to obtain the necessary subsidies for the school, to find money, paints, and material. I have to apply to the authorities countless times so that my pupils can be freed from military service. I was constantly on the move. My wife acted on my behalf in my absence. I went to the meetings of the Gubispolkom (Russian abbreviation for "government-Soviet") to apply for loans from the city ..."

But ingratitude is the reward. The pupils partly took advantage of his good nature, and the tutors could not or did not want to keep up with his working pace. Their enthusiasm slackened while Chagall's remained unbroken. His patience was hard tried. Many mocked the meetings which he called in his "status as chairman" and which often dragged on late into the night. They mocked the school and scoffed at Chagall and his views. Eventually it came to serious differences of opinion between him and Malevitsch — and in Chagall's absence — to a teachers' revolt which the pupils were also drawn into.

After this Chagall turned his back on the academy. He was embittered since he had neglected his work for years so that he could devote himself completely to the tasks in his native country. Now he was forced to realize that his commitment was expected of him but was not seriously acknowledged. "it should not surprise me if my city obliterates all traces of me after some time and does not remember the person who abandoned his paintbrush, who tortured himself, suffered and tried to give art a home here, who dreamed of changing ordinary houses into museums and common citizens into artists. And then I realized that a prophet is never accepted in his own country. I left for Moscow ..."

Moscow was again the capital since 1918. In 1919, the government bought 12 paintings from the artist. But still Chagall had trouble providing for his wife and his daughter. The financial means were once again missing. The offer to make the murals, decorations, and costumes for the city's "Jewish Theatre" therefore came just in time. At the same time it was the fulfillment of a long-cherished desire since he had always had a liking for the theatre. "One proposed that I make the murals in the reception halls and the stage decorations for the first play. 'Ah!' I thought, 'that is the opportunity to change the old Jewish theatre radically, its psychological naturalism, its stuck-on beards. Here, at least on the walls I will be able to express myself to my heart's content and freely design everything which appears to me to be indispensable for the renewal of the national theatre' ... For the main wall I created a painting 'Introduction to the New Folk Theatre'. The other partition-walls, the ceiling, and the friezes represented the ancestors of the present-day actors — a folk-musician, a wedding-comedian, a dancing woman, a Torah-scribe as the first dream-poet, and finally a modern couple who swirl across the stage. Prepared food, pretzels, and fruit on a set table decorated the friezes ..."

Chagall was in his element. He enjoyed the work, enjoyed the theatre atmosphere and the good harmony with the actors and actresses who appreciated him a lot and who sometimes gave him some bread or soup. Meanwhile he had moved his family to the country. They lived in the small village of Malachovka, not far from Moscow. He visited them as often as he was able to. When his theatre commission was accomplished he moved there as well in 1921 as an art master.

The children who had been given a new home in the war orphans' colony of Malachovka and who were now to be taught by him had been through terrible times. Their fate moved Chagall deeply. He was glad that he could help to bring a little light into the existence of those poor creatures with his art teaching. He called them the "unhappiest of orphans". Chagall loved them all and was pleased by their enthusiasm and desire for knowledge. "... They rush at the colours like wild animals rush at meat. One of these boys seemed to be in a constant creative ecstasy. He painted, composed, and wrote verse. Another constructed his works of art calmly like an engineer. Some of them concerned themselves with abstract art and thus established connections with Cimabue and the art of church windows. For a long time I was fascinated with their drawings, with this inspired stammering, till the time came when I had to leave them ...", he tells in his memoirs which he started to write then in Malachovka.

In the long run, Chagall's fatherland did not seem to be the right place for him. He felt hampered in his artistic freedom. Art was influenced too much by politics which appeared to the individualist which he was as a kind of strait-jacket. "... For me, a picture has to contain elements of my conception of painting. Man is looking for something new; he has to discover the origin of his own language time and time again — a language like that of primitive people, of people who open their mouths for the first time to speak the one and only truth. For me a picture is an area, covered with representations of things (objects, animals, human

Table III

The Teaching of Philetas
From the cycle Daphne and Chloe. 1961
Colour lithograph, 42 x 32 cm

forms) in a certain order, in which logic and illustration have no place. Perhaps there exists a secret fourth or fifth dimension (not just for the eye) which intuitively creates a series of graphic and psychic objects, which opens the viewer's eyes to new and strange conceptions. And neither the so-called 'real' colours nor 'conventional' colours depict the object in its reality. What is called perspective is unnecessary to give the picture depth. Life itself creates opposites without which art would be unimaginable and incomplete."

His finances did not look good either. He literally had to run after his payment for the murals. Time and time again, he was consoled and then had to come away empty-handed. Finally he had enough. He thought about his "pre-war paintings" which had remained in Berlin and Paris. Would it not be sensible to build up a career there? On top of this a German friend wrote to him from Germany, "... Do you know that you are famous here? Your paintings have founded expressionism. They are changing hands for a lot of money." But he added, "Do not rely on the money which Walden owes you. He will not pay you anything, he maintains that fame is enough for you."

After the decision had been made to travel to Germany, Chagall applied for exit permits for himself and his family. They arrived in Berlin in the summer of 1922. To his joy he discovered that he really was not unknown there. Herwarth Walden had sold his pictures — approximately 150 — and these had laid the foundation for his fame in the West. The money from the sale had been paid into a bank by Walden, but in the meantime it had become worthless due to inflation.

Chagall had no other choice but to fight for his rights. The legal action brought about the return of several of his works, but this was just a drop in the bucket.

The artist stayed in Berlin for a year and ventured into a field which he had disregarded till that time — prints. That he suddenly discovered his love for this section of art can be mainly attributed to the art dealer and editor Paul Cassirer and his partner Walter Feilchenfeldt who commissioned Chagall to illustrate his autobiography "My Life" with his own etchings. Before Chagall could begin with the work he had to learn the necessary techniques. For this reason he took lessons with Hermann Struck, one of the best tutors in this field. Many famous artists had emanated from his school. In his handbook "The Art of Etching", Struck did not leave unmentioned the esteem which he had for his pupil. In this book he describes Chagall as "the most powerful symbol of artistic and spiritual evolution of young Russia. A wild enthusiast," he wrote, "who quickly storms through all phases with the unconscious strength of the genius; from the naturalistic amassing of everyday occurences surrounding him to the mystical creating ..."

Chagall who was fascinated by the new possibilities, which were available to him now, created — as he had learned the different techniques of printing — not just etchings but also woodcuts and lithographs in considerable quantity. Because of difficulties in translation, the publication of his autobiography "My Life" was only realized in Paris in 1931 after Bella Chagall had translated the text into French. But already in 1923 a portfolio with twenty dry-point sheets and etchings was published in Berlin under the same title by Paul Cassirer.

From that time on, graphical art played a major role in the artist's work and was instrumental in his rise to fame. Chagall connected his graphic work to his painting just as the other way round his painting was linked with the experiences which he gained from his graphic work. The one profited, as it were, from the other.

News of his ability soon spread to Paris and to the ears of Ambroise Vollard, the famous art dealer, who commissioned Chagall in autumn 1923 to illustrate "Dead Souls" by Gogol, an extensive task which stretched over years. The artist left Germany and returned to his beloved Paris where he took up quarters in the Avenue d'Orléans with his wife and daughter.

A happy period with no financial worries began, especially as the co-operation with Vollard proved to be very productive. While Chagall was still occupied with "Dead Souls", the art dealer entrusted him with an equally complicated task, the illustration to La Fontaine's "Fables". He had imagined colour etchings in the manner of those from the 18th century. They were to be made from gouache paintings by Chagall in a studio especially furnished by Vollard for this undertaking under the supervision of the copper printer Maurice Potin. The first test prints satisfied neither the artist nor the client so that both eventually agreed to do without colour and decided on a black and white edition instead. This, however, was only published in 1952 by Tériade in Paris, thirteen years after Vollard's death.

Vollard did not live to see the completion of the bible illustrations either with which he had commissioned Chagall in 1930. The work on this monumental task took almost a quarter of a century, and the result certainly represents the zenith of Chagall's graphical creations. "The bible had fascinated me since I was a child," he explained, "I still believe that the bible is the most wide-ranging source ever for poetic art. I have always drawn from it in life and in art. A bible is like an echo from nature. I have attempted to convey this secret. For me, these paintings do not just represent the dream of a people but rather the dreams of mankind."

In order that he could understand and interpret biblical events better he travelled to Palestine, Syria, and Egypt in 1931 — before starting his work — and visited all the places which are mentioned in the Old Testament. He returned, impressed, to France two months later.

Considering the scale of Vollard's commissions for illustrations one has to ask oneself how Chagall found the time to achieve the masterly accomplishments in painting like "Rural Life" (1925), "Childhood Memories" (1925), "The Three Acrobats" (1926), or "The Lovers in the Lilac Bush" (1930), to mention just a few. But Chagall was a person who could never take a rest. He is often supposed to have said that he would die on the day on which he stopped working. The fact that he reached the ripe old age of 98 and was able to be productive until the end could have been the reward for this attitude towards life.

Flowers, lovers, and the circus world belonged to his favourite themes in the thirties. He had long been impressed by the colourful life of acrobats and clowns, but he only began to involve himself artistically with the theme in 1926. Numerous oil paintings as well as one circus portfolio with 19 gouache paintings — still commissioned by Vollard — bear witness to his close alliance with the circus folk whom he so admired. "I have always regarded clowns, acrobats, and actors as tragic individuals who in my eyes are similar to the people in certain religious scenes. Even today when I paint a crucifixion or another religious picture, I have almost the same feelings as in those days when I painted the circus folk. And still there is nothing 'literary' in these paintings, and it is difficult to explain why I discover a psycho-plastic similarity between these two types of composition." (1948)

The cow almost appears to be a leitmotif in numerous works by Chagall, sometimes put in as if by incident, sometimes as an eye-catcher. "I have often been asked why I have painted so many cows. It seems as if the cow made world politics then. Cubism chopped it in bits, expressionism distorted it ..."

In 1937, Chagall became a French citizen. He had spent approximately a third of his life in France by that time, and he loved the country. Once, when he was asked whether he felt like a Russian-Jewish artist, he answered, "In art there is no nationalism. I bear Russia in my heart but without France I would not be Chagall." Undoubtedly a wise statement.

Retrospective exhibitions in Paris and Basel and an individual exhibition in New York had made his name widely known. He had long become a respected person.

In the meantime though, there was a growing unrest in the world, the Second World War was imminent. The fate of his Jewish fellow believers who were mercilessly persecuted by the National Socialists affected him deeply and influenced his work. The cheerfulness which had determined the general tone up until then was replaced by a dramatic mood. Works such as "The White Crucifixion" (1938) were created, works in which he interpreted world matters in a religious manner, and in which he focused the crucifixion as a symbol of Jewish suffering.

His fame fortunately saved him, when eventually European ground threatened to get too hot for him and the danger of being handed over to the Germans existed. He was able to leave the country just in time on May 7th, 1941 in answer to an invitation from the Museum of Modern Art in New York. On June 23rd he arrived in New York with his family and was in safety.

During the summer months of 1942, Chagall worked in Mexico on the scenery and costumes for the Tchaikovsky ballet "Aleko" which enjoyed great success at its première in Mexico City on September 10th of that year. The critics said, "Chagall turns out to be the hero of the evening. He has painted four magnificent coulisses with his own hands which are not really good stage settings at all but rather wonderful works of art. They are so exciting that one wishes that all the people on stage would not constantly block ones view ..."

On September 2nd, 1944, the artist was hit by a severe blow of fate: Bella died as the result of a virus infection. Chagall who had drawn a great deal of his creative power from an extremely happy marriage felt burnt out as a result of this and was unable to paint for months. His old energy returned very slowly and with it the desire to work. With nostalgic memories of Bella, he made paintings like "Wedding Lights" or others which were concerned with her death. In 1945 he took a commission from the Metropolitan Opera for the decoration of Stravinsky's ballett "The Firebird". In the following year he set foot on French soil again for the first time since he had left. In 1948, he finally moved back to his adopted country. He lived first in the vicinity of Paris and shortly after in Saint-Jean-Cap-Ferrat on the Côte d'Azur until he finally settled in Vence.

After the war, Chagall exhibitions took place in New York, Paris, Amsterdam, and London, followed by others in Zurich, Bern, Jerusalem, and in many other cities and countries. In 1948

Table IV

Winter
From the cycle Daphne and Chloe. 1961
Colour lithograph, 42 x 32 cm

he was awarded the first prize for graphics at the 25th Biennial in Venice, from London he received the commission to make the murals for the Watergate Theatre.

He was happy again, not just in his work but also in his private life. On July 12th, 1952 Chagall married his fellow Russian Valentina Brodsky whom he lovingly called "Vava" and who stood by him — as Bella had once done — as a good angel, Muse, critic, and partner.

Meanwhile he also occupied himself with ceramics, sculptures, and mosaics and discovered his love for glass painting. In his later years he was one of the most sought after glass painters of his time. He created, for example, artistic windows for the cathedral in Metz, for the synagogue of the Hadassah university clinic in Jerusalem, the Minster of Our Lady in Zurich, and for the cathedral in Reims. In 1962, he received an especially honourable commission. Chagall related, "At the start of the sixties the Minister of Culture André Malraux suggested that I should renew the old ceiling in the Paris Opera House. I was dismayed, touched, and moved. Dismayed because I am frightened of commissions although secretly I dream of monumental works. Touched by the trust which André Malraux had in me. I had doubts about myself, about my work, and certain opinions strengthened these doubts until one day my wife said to me, 'Make a few sketches, then you will see for yourself' ... I thought of the Opera House as a complete work of art. I wanted to reflect as if in a mirror the communal dreams and the creativity of the actors and musicians. To sing like a bird. To honour the distinguished opera and ballet composers."

He succeeded eminently in all of this. A colourful masterpiece of breathtaking beauty burst into blossom. Chagall, a good friend of music, who especially liked to paint to the sound of Mozart all his life, had taken on the commission under just one condition: he did not want any payment for it.

During his life, Chagall received innumerable honours, for example, in 1959 he was awarded an honorary doctor's title from Glasgow University, and in 1977 — from the French President's hand — the Grand Cross of the Legion of Honour, France's highest award. In spite of all this, the artist remained modest all his life. He came from humble origins and gratefully accepted the fame and everything that went along with it and was happy about it. His personality was not altered by it at all. "As everybody knows, a good person can be a bad artist. But no one can become an artist who is not a great personality and therefore not a 'good person'," he once said. He was the best example for the truth of this statement.

Of course there were also adversaries who criticized his art and who said that he was "mystical and poetical". Chagall never had too much to say, at least not when it concerned the interpretation of his work, but every now and then he felt compelled to clear up some misunderstanding. So he said in 1947, "My pictures do not contain any fairy stories, nor tales or folktales. I am against terms such as 'imagination' and 'symbolism'. Our whole inner world is reality — perhaps even more real than the visible world. To describe everything which appears to be illogical as imagination or fairy-tale means nothing else than admitting that one does not understand nature. I have used cows, milkmaids, hens, and Russian architecture in the country as sources of form because they are a part of the country from which I come, and undoubtedly they have left a deeper impression in my visual memory than all the other impressions which have been bestowed on me. Every artist is born in some place, and even later, when he reacts to the impression of other surroundings, a certain essence, a certain aroma of his homeland will always remain in his work."

Another time he declared, "When in my paintings I cut off the cow's head and put it back on the wrong way round or sometimes paint the whole picture the other way round, I did not do this to make literature. I want to bring a psychic shock into my work which is always motivated by pictorial reasons, in other words: a fourth dimension. So where I am concerned one should not speak any more of fairy-stories, of the fantastic, of Chagall the flying artist. I am a painter who is unconsciously conscious."

This rich artistic life came to an end in the evening of March 28th, 1985. Shortly before Chagall had still painted on a self-portrait in the studio of his house in Saint-Paul-de-Vence. He was the last great painter of his time and — as the art historian Georg Schmidt from Basel had once so fittingly expressed — "an undeserved present to our century."

ILLUSTRATIONS

Me and the Village. 1911
Oil on canvas, 191 x 150.5 cm
Museum of Modern Art, New York

The Violinist. 1911

Oil on canvas, 94.5 x 69.5 cm
Kunstsammlung Nordrhein Westfalen, Dusseldorf

The Poet Mazin. 1911/12

Oil on canvas, 73 x 54 cm
Collection Ida Meyer-Chagall, Basel

29

A Spoonful of Milk. 1912
Oil on canvas, 38 x 31 cm
Private collection, Basel

The Pinch of Snuff. 1912

Oil on canvas, 128 x 90 cm
Private collection

The Burning House. 1913

Oil on canvas, 107.2 x 120.5 cm
Solomon R. Guggenheim Museum, New York

The Jew in Red. 1914
Oil on cardboard, mounted, 100 x 80 cm
Collection Charles im Obersteg, Geneva

Selfportrait. 1914

Oil on pasteboard, mounted, 54 x 38 cm
Collection Charles im Obersteg, Geneva

The News-Vendor. 1914

Oil on canvas, 98 x 78.5 cm
Private collection, Paris

Praying Jew. 1914
(The Rabbi from Witebsk)
Oil on canvas, 104 x 84 cm
Museo d'Arte Moderna, Venice

The Jew in Green. 1914

Oil on cardboard, 100 x 80 cm
Collection Charles im Obersteg, Geneva

The Birthday. 1915
Oil on cardboard, 80.5 x 99.5 cm
Museum of Modern Art, New York

The Red Gate. 1917

Oil on cardboard, 49 x 66.5 cm
Staatsgalerie, Stuttgart

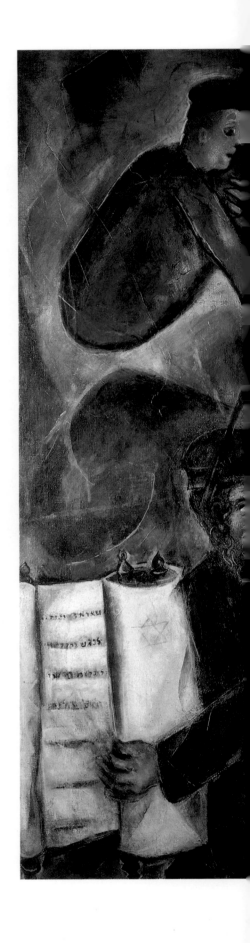

The Fall of the Angel. 1923/33/47

Oil on canvas, 148 x 189 cm
Kunstmuseum, Basel

51

Bride with a Bunch of Flowers. 1926

Oil on canvas, 69 x 55 cm
Städtische Kunsthalle, Mannheim

The Church of Chambon. 1926

Gouache on paper, 65 x 51 cm
Museum Boymans-van Beuningen, Rotterdam

The Female Acrobat. 1926/27

Oil on canvas, 116 x 90 cm
Private collecton, Basel

The Female Acrobat. 1930

Oil on canvas, 65 x 32 cm
Centre National G. Pompidou, Paris

The Blue Donkey. Around 1930
Oil on canvas, 16 x 24.5 cm
Hoffmann Stiftung, Kunstmuseum, Basel

The Bride and Bridegroom. 1930

Oil on canvas, 80 x 110 cm
Private collection

Bonjour Paris. 1939-42

Oil and crayon on cardboard, 62 x 46 cm
Private collection, Paris

The Juggler. 1943
Oil on canvas, 109 x 79 cm
Mrs. Gilbert Chapman Foundation
The Art Institute, Chicago

67

The Sledge. 1943

Gouache and crayon, 51 x 76 cm
Private collection

Rural Scene. 1944

Gouache and crayon, 46 x 48 cm
Private collection

The Wedding. 1944

Oil on canvas, 99 x 74 cm
Collection Ida Meyer-Chagall, Basel

At Dusk. 1944

Oil on canvas, 100 x 73 cm
Private collection, Bern

Blue Landscape. 1949

Gouache, 79 x 57 cm
Von der Heydt-Museum, Wuppertal

Sun and Mimosas. 1949
Gouache, 79 x 57 cm
Von der Heydt-Museum, Wuppertal

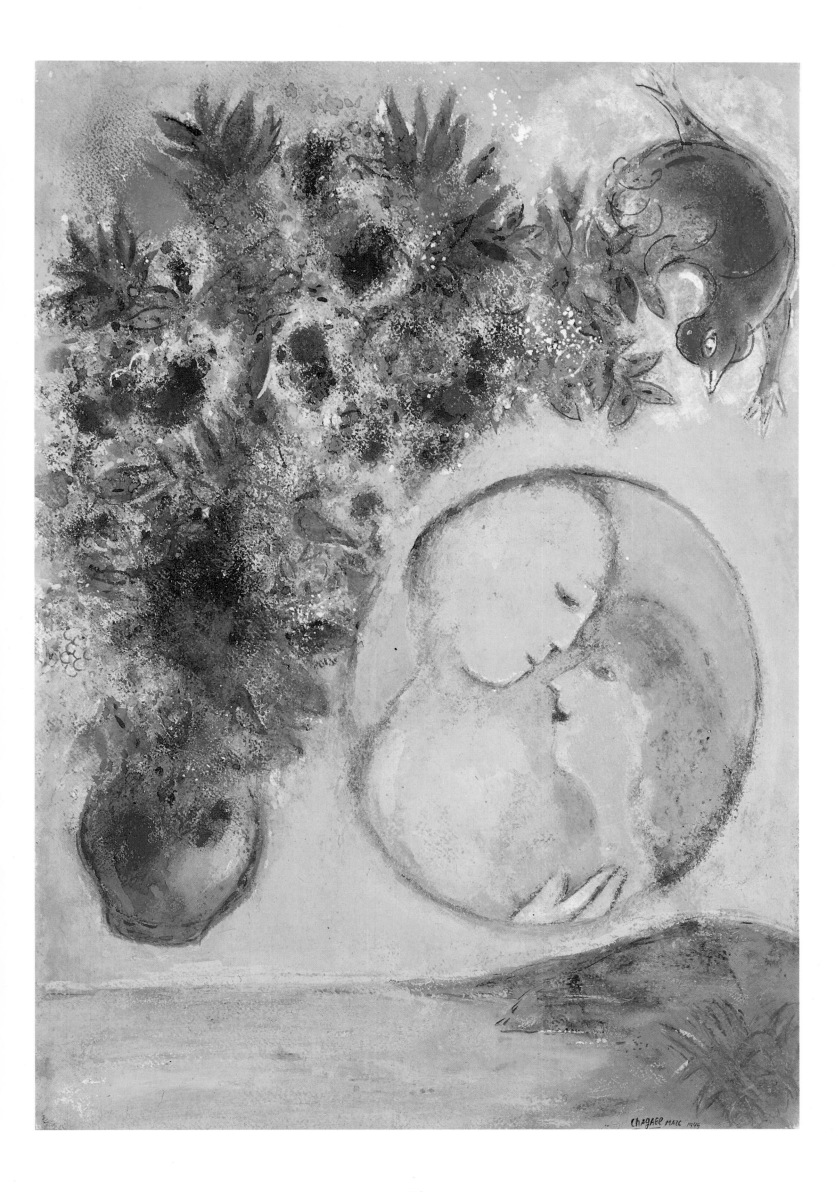

Still Life with Flowers. 1949

Gouache on cardboard, 78.5 x 57.5 cm
Von der Heydt-Museum, Wuppertal

The Green Night. 1952
Oil on canvas, 72 x 60 cm
Private collection, Switzerland

The Seine Bridges. 1954
Oil on canvas, 111.5 x 163.5 cm
Kunsthalle, Hamburg

The Field of Mars. 1954/55

Oil on canvas, 149.5 x 105 cm
Museum Folkwang, Essen

The Red House. 1955

Oil on canvas, 59 x 51.3 cm
Kunsthalle, Hanover

The White Window. 1955

Gouache, 150 x 119.5 cm
Private collection

Le Visiteur. 1956

Gouache, 54 x 46 cm
Private collection

The Tree Jesse. 1960
Oil on canvas, 150 x 120 cm
Private collection, Basel

95

The Lovers. 1963
Gouache, 51 x 52 cm
Private collection, Basel

The Bouquet. 1967/68

Oil on canvas, 65 x 92 cm
Private collection

Horsewoman with Doves. 1970

Gouache and crayon, 51 x 75 cm
Private collection

Villagers. 1979
Oil on canvas, 81.5 x 87 cm
Private collection, Basel

CHRONOLOGY

1887   Marc Chagall was born in Witebsk on July 7th. He comes from an ordinary Jewish family.

1906   He terminates the parish school and takes lessons with Jehuda Pen, a painter who had studied at the academy of St Petersburg.

1907   The young man ventures a move to St Petersburg and begins to study at the School of the Imperial Committee for the Promotion of Art.

1908   After a short time Chagall realizes that he will not learn at the official school what he regards as necessary to become an artist. He attends the Saidenberg School for a few months but then changes to Léon Bakst in the Svanseva School. The work with Bakst is a liberation for him. At the same time he realizes, and Bakst encourages him in his views, that his artistic future lies in Paris.

1909   He meets his later wife Bella Rosenfeld.

1910   In summer Chagall travels to Paris. He finds his first studio in Impasse du Maine. He makes friends, has contact with artists and intellectuals. Blaise Cendrars, Max Jacob, Apollinaire, Léger, Modigliani are among his friends.

1911   He is able to obtain a larger studio in the Ruche, an artists' quarter.

1912   He takes part in exhibitions with his paintings for the first time in the Salon des Indépendants and in the Salon d'Automne.

1913   He has his first contact with Germany: his friend Apollinaire introduces him to Herwarth Walden who is impressed by the works of the young Russian artist and organizes

1914   the first exhibition by Chagall in the gallery DER STURM in Berlin. Chagall travels to the opening, then on to Russia where Bella is waiting for him.

1915   Marc Chagall marries the sweetheart of his youth, Bella. It is a war-wedding: Russia is at war, Chagall cannot leave the country. His first exhibition takes place in Moscow.

1916   A great exhibition is organized in Moscow. His daughter Ida is born.

1917   After the October Revolution the Chagall family moves back to Witebsk.

1918 Chagall is appointed Commissioner for the Fine Arts in the previous district of Witebsk. In this capacity he organizes the festivities for the commemoration of the October Revolution.

1919 Chagall achieves the founding of the academy under his direction. But already after a few months there are disagreements with the colleagues who he had appointed. Chagall resigns.

1920 He moves to Moscow, works for the Jewish Theatre, where he designs the murals, stage-curtains, and costumes.

1921 He works as a drawing teacher in the war-orphans colony Malachovska near Moscow.

1922 Chagall leaves Russia. First he goes to Berlin where he had left pictures before the war. However, these had been sold, the money from the sale is mostly devalued by inflation. But contact with Bruno Cassirer is of decisive importance. He draws Chagall's attention to the possibilities offered by graphic printing and introduces him to the engraver Hermann Struck with whom Chagall works. So the start of Chagall's rich graphic work lies in Berlin.

1923 Chagall moves to Paris. He gets to know Ambroise Vollard who commissions him to illustrate Gogol's "Dead Souls".

1924 The first large retrospective exhibition in Paris in the Galerie Barbazanges-Hodebert.

1926 The Reinhart Galleries in New York hold the first Chagall exhibition with great success. The gouache paintings to the fables by La Fontaine are made.

1927 Vollard commissions him to make a portfolio of circus representations. The gouache paintings for Cirque Vollard are made. In the following year

1928 work begins on the etchings which drags on until 1931.

1929 The French edition of Chagall's memoirs is published after the original Russian version proved to be almost untranslatable. "Ma Vie" is published.

1931 In the same year Chagall travels to Palastine for the first time in preparation for the planned bible illustrations. Work on this goes on until 1939 and then again from 1952 till 1956.

1933 The great retrospective exhibition in the Kunsthalle in Basel takes place. In the following years Chagall undertakes a series of travels, he visits Spain, Poland, and Italy.

1939 Chagall receives the Carnegie Prize. An invitation from the Museum of Modern Art in New York occasions a journey to America which takes place in 1941.

1941 Because of the war situation and the German invasion of France a return there is unthinkable. Chagall settles in America. The Galerie Pierre Matisse holds regular exhibitions.

1942 Summer stay in Mexico. Stage-settings and costumes for the ballet "Aleko" from the piece for three pianos by Tchaikovsky.

1944 Death of his wife Bella.

1945 Chagall accepts the commission for stage settings and costumes for the ballet "The Firebird" by Igor Stravinsky in the New York Metropolitan Opera.

1946 Chagall moves to High Falls. The Museum of Modern Art stages a large retrospective exhibition which is later shown in the Art Institute in Chicago.

1947 The Musée d'Art Moderne in Paris shows the first large retrospective exhibition in Europe followed by the Stedelijk Museum, Amsterdam, and the Tate Gallery, London.

1948 Chagall moves back to France for good. First he settles in Orgeval near St Germain-en Laye. The "Arabian Nights" are made. The considerable lithographic postwar creativeness begins with them. He gets to know Aimé Maeght who becomes his art dealer. The publisher Tériade publishes the "Dead Souls".

1949 He paints murals for the Watergate Theatre in London. He prefers to live in the South and buys a home in Vence. In Antibes and Vallauris he dedicates himself to ceramic work.

1950 Chagall finally settles in Vence. There he often meets Matisse and Picasso who live in Nice and Vallauris respectively. He designs a placard for an exhibition by Maeght which is printed by Fernand Moulot. From now on almost all of Chagall's lithographs are printed in this printing-press. Large exhibitions are staged in Munich, Zurich, and Bern.

1952 Marriage to Valentine (Vava) Brodsky. A trip to Greece serves as preparation for the work on Daphne and Chloe, a sequence of lithographs. The fables by La Fontaine are published by Tériade.

1953 Chagall begins working on the legendary sequence of Paris paintings.

1954 Immediately after a second trip to Greece the artist begins to work intensively on Daphne and Chloe. The graphic series is printed

1957 in the Mourlot printing-press. In the same year the Chagall House is opened in Haifa while the Bibliothèque Nationale in Paris stages a large exhibition of Chagall's graphic work.

1958 The artist creates the decoration (stage-setting and costumes) for Ravel's ballet Daphne and Chloe. As well as this the designs are finished for the stained-glass windows of the cathedral in Metz. A trip to Chicago.

1959 Glasgow University awards Chagall an honorary doctor's title which the artist accepts personally. He is also appointed as honorary member of the American Academy of Arts and Letters. In Paris, in the Musée des Arts Décoratifs a large exhibition takes place, there are also exhibitions in Munich and Hamburg. Chagall paints a large mural for the Schauspielhaus in Frankfort.

1960 He receives another honorary doctor's title, this time from the U.S.A., from the Brandeis University. In Copenhagen he receives the Erasmus Prize of the European Cultural Foundation together with Oskar Kokoschka. Chagall's involvement in Israel is continued with 12 magnificent windows for the synagogue of the Hadassah university clinic near Jerusalem. The first window for the cathedral in Metz is also finished. The glass work for the cathedrals is the theme of an exhibition in the Reims museum.

1964 Chagall travels to the United Nations in New York to the inauguration of a window which he had created in memory of Dag Hammarsjöld. Many designs for glass windows and other official commissions for the public follow in the next years. Some of the more spectacular are the ceiling paintings for the Grand Opéra in Paris and wall decorations for the New Metropolitan Opera House in New York for which he also designs the decorations and costumes of Mozart's Zauberflöte for the opening presentation.

1967 The New York Opera House is ceremoniously opened. Large retrospectve exhibitions are staged for the artist's 80th birthday in Zurich and Cologne as well as a Hommage à Chagall in the Fondation Maeght in Saint-Paul-de-Vence. The Louvre shows the exhibition 'Biblical Gospel', a donation from Marc and Vava Chagall.

1973 In summer the Musée National du Message Biblique Marc Chagall is ceremoniously opened by André Malraux in Nice. This great foundation becomes a central museum event. Russia also takes official notice of the great artist now. At the invitation of the Soviet Minister of Culture Chagall travels to Russia where he visits Moscow and Leningrad, while an exhibition of his work is on show in the Tretjakov Gallery.

1977 Chagall is awarded the Grand Cross of the Legion of Honour. Jerusalem appoints him honorary citizen, an exhibition in the Louvre is opened by the French president.

1984 The last great memorable exhibition of Chagall's work in his lifetime is staged. The theme of the show in the Musée d'Art Moderne in Paris is called Work on Paper.

1985 Marc Chagall dies in his house in Saint-Paul-de-Vence.

TABLE OF ILLUSTRATIONS

Reproductionrights Marc Chagall: © VG Bild-Kunst, Bonn, 1988

Photographic acknowledgements:
Colorphoto Hans Hinz SWB, CH-Allschwill: S. 25, 27, 29, 31, 33, 35,37, 39, 41, 43, 45, 47, 51, 57, 61, 63, 65, 67, 69, 71, 73, 75, 83, 91.
Dr. Roland Doschka, Rottenburg-Dettingen: S. 97, 99, 101, 103, Tf. I, Tf. II, Tf. III, Tf. IV.